Heartbreak Therapy

D. Foy Hutchins

Copyright © 2015 D. Foy Hutchins
All rights reserved. No part of this book may be reproduced, scanned, or distributed in any printed or electronic form without permission.
First Edition: December 2015
Printed in the United States of America
ISBN 10: 151976569X
ISBN 13: 9781519765697

To the wonderful people of the Galilee Church,

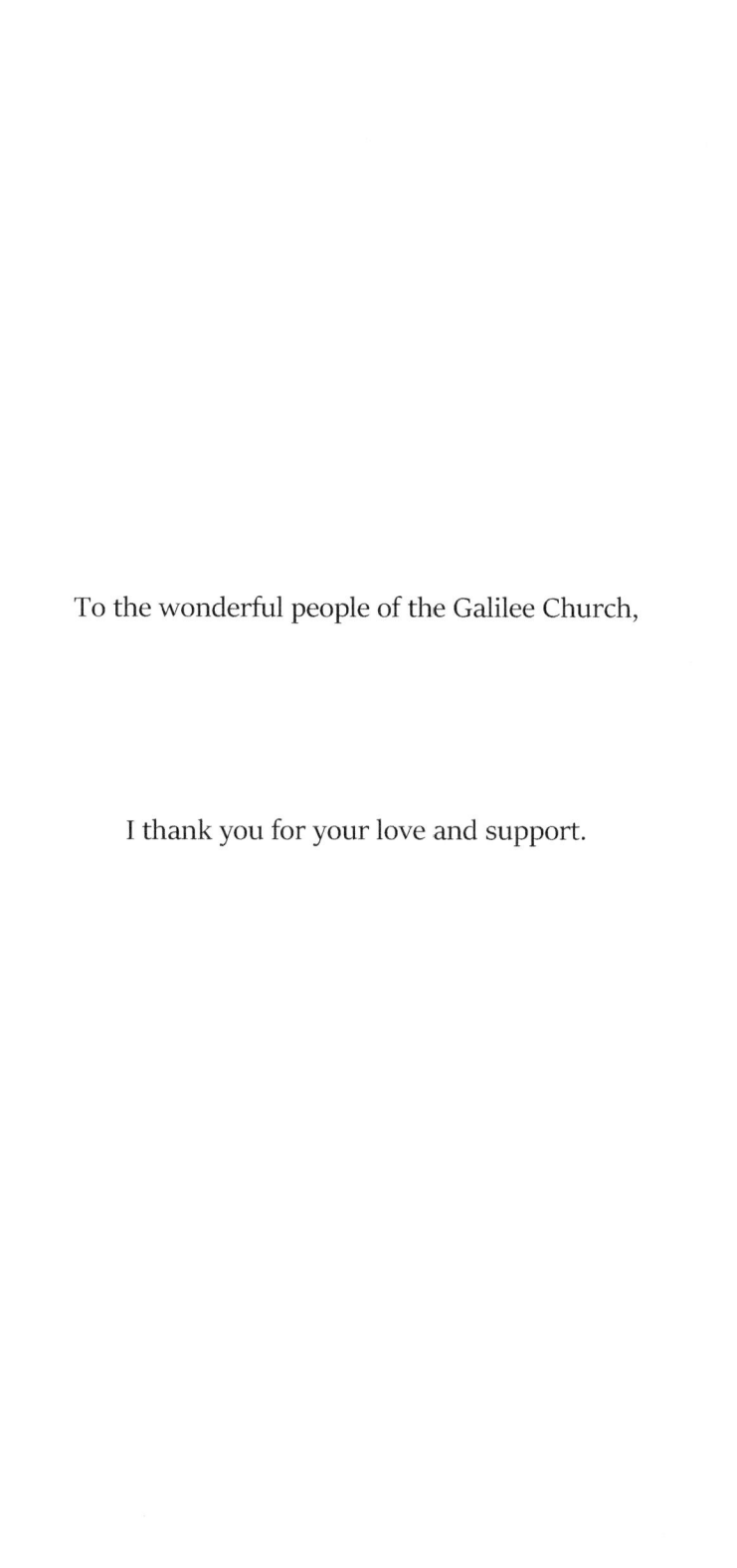

I thank you for your love and support.

D Foy Hutchins

TABLE OF CONTENTS

ACKNOWLEDGEMENTS VI

CHAPTER 1: LOSING WEIGHT 1

CHAPTER 2: YOU ARE NOT ALONE 17

CHAPTER 3: HALF FULL 29

CHAPTER 4: NO MORE SLAVES 47

CHAPTER 5: GRATITUDE 59

CHAPTER 6: PROCEED WITH CAUTION 65

CHAPTER 7: DO SOMETHING DEEPER 71

CHAPTER 8: LAS VEGAS 81

CHAPTER 9: RELAX, RESET, RECOVER 93

Acknowledgements

It is a true saying, tough times reveal who your true friends are.

Divorce is a difficult journey, no matter who you are. Although simplified by terms like filing date, finalized date, court dates, dissolution agreements, separation period, etc., a stroke of a pen doesn't stop the emotional roller coaster from rolling. It's a journey.

I am eternally grateful for the people that have shared this time with me. I had no idea how blessed I was to have these people in my life. Anyone can applaud you when things go well, but only unconditional love can ease the pains of failure.

I thank those who have kept me laughing, supplied my comfort food, motivated me, prayed earnestly for me, supported my ministry, endured my rambling, dried my tears, forgave my mistakes, understood my frustration, held my hand, lifted my countenance, stood by my side, sharpened my focus, rekindled my drive, shown me real love, and challenged me to overcome.

My parents have shown an extra-special love. There could not have been a better couple to raise me. From training me up as a child to picking me up as a man, Ron and Sabrina Hutchins have been my champions.

Proverbs 17:17 states "a friend loves at all times and a brother is born from adversity." God has blessed me with two outstanding biological brothers: La'Ron and Ja'Quaylen. What an inspiration they have been throughout my difficult transition. When I think of them, I smile and I am encouraged to be the best role-model I can be.

Outside of my siblings, Melvin Andrew Davis has been a brother in the truest sense. Only once in my life have I made a three o'clock in the morning distress call and you were that one. I could call on you to pray for me in a way that no one else in my life could. I cherish your friendship. You are one of the greatest people I know.

Louis R. Jones has also been a brother beloved. At one point, I was between a rock and a hard place. This brother welcomed me into his home and treated me like I was blood. I wish one day I can be half as generous to some young preacher as you have meant to me.

Finally, to these three couples, I thank you for showing me that an endless love is still possible: Elliott and Virginia Cuff, Louis and Curtrina Jones, and Vincent and Connie Perkins. The way you love gives me hope. After spending time with each of you, I want to fall in love all over again. Your examples have helped my heart heal. The best is yet to come!

Chapter 1

Losing Weight

"...let us lay aside every weight, and the sin which doth so easily beset us, and let us run with patience the race that is set before us" Hebrews 12:1

As a teenager, like many young boys I enjoyed playing sports, basketball was my favorite. I attended Livingston High School where the basketball program had a rich and proud tradition. Now I was not a star player, but I was glad to be on a winning team. Those were good times. For me, the practices were more enjoyable than the games. There, we got to show our new skills to our peers. When I first got the urge to dunk, I was a freshman on the junior varsity team. I had this teammate, he was a sophomore at the time but he towered over six feet. We called him "Droop." Droop could jump. When he dunked, his head almost touched the rim. I wanted to get up like that.

Without the natural ability and height he possessed, I researched how my vertical leap could increase. If not as high as Droop's, then at least high enough to dunk with both hands. You know, impress the guys at practice, show off in front of the coaches, and possibly get more playing time.

I bought special workout shoes and exercise videos to help increase my vertical leap. One video was called "Air Alert." I did that video every day after school and continued the workouts during summer break. I wanted be able to dunk when the new season rolled around. Although my legs got stronger and I was able to jump higher, I still couldn't dunk.

The best advice I got was that the fastest way to jump higher was to lose weight. Now I was always somewhat slim. So I didn't have much weight to lose. But I was suffering from a honey-bun addiction. Little Debbie was my first love. I ate a honey bun before school and one after. Almost five hundred calories each! I figured if I stopped eating those honey buns, I could lose a little weight, which would lead to achieving my goal of dunking.

It worked. After losing just seven pounds, I dunked a regulation height goal in my front yard at home. With great anticipation, I wanted to get the park that next Sunday! Sunday afternoon came. I gathered the guys around the goal line to watch. I stood at the three-point line, threw the ball up for the perfect bounce, ran up to the rim with confidence and dunked in front of my friends. What a feeling.

I kept exercising that summer and stayed away from the honey buns. When tryouts came for basketball season, I dunked, impressed the coaches, and I made the team. In practice, I watched Droop dunk with his usual flare. But this time, I noticed something I had overlooked before. Droop was the skinniest guy in the gym! Maybe Droop could jump so high because his frame was so light.

To understand this principle is worth the entire book. Heartbreak, disappointment, hurt and pain hinder you from reaching God's best for your life. If you really want to get up, you have to let some stuff go. The lighter you are, the higher you can rise.

Forgiveness is the First Step

When you hold a grudge against someone or carry resentment for what was done to you, you are carrying around excess weight. Therefore, no matter how strong you are or how hard you work, that extra pressure will hinder you from reaching your full potential.

Years ago the world lost one of the most beautiful and talented singers of our time, Aaliyah. While flying on a private jet, her plane experienced engine failure and crashed because they were carrying too much baggage.

Too much weight can bring you down.

Life is hard enough. Job says we are here on earth for a few days and those days are full of trouble (Job 14:1 paraphrased). The reason you should learn to forgive others is because life is too short to walk around hating someone else. You only have a few days here. Why waste that precious time hating someone else. Also, those few days are already full of trouble. Why let unforgiveness cause more trouble to add to the trouble you already have?

No matter who you are, gravity affects us all the same. All objects fall to the earth at 9.8 m/s^2. There is a force that pulls us down and keeps us down. Along with gravity, you have your own physical load. However much you weigh, you carry that. Even those in the top physical shape are limited by gravity and are wearied by their own physicality. The strongest man in the world can lift five pounds possibly hundreds of times, but sooner or later, it will wear him down. It's the same way with our spiritual and emotional lives.

There is but so much you can carry before it breaks you. The strongest people have a breaking point and I've learned not to test my limits. As soon as you are offended, hurt, or disappointed, you have to let it go. The sooner, the better. Otherwise, it will render you weak and ineffective.

I had a choice to make. Should I waste precious time with perpetual fury, aiming at a target that was already long gone? Or should I begin a new journey, aiming at new goals that were centered around my purpose and prosperity? The choice was clear, I had to separate yesterday's pain from tomorrow's possibilities. I had to forgive.

The first person I had to forgive was myself. After we lose someone or something, we tend to self-analyze. You ask yourself, "Did I say everything I could have said? Why didn't I do more? Maybe things would be different if I had done better. Was it my fault?"

Truth is, you're not incorrect but you're incomplete. It is important to self-reflect and learn from the mistakes of your past. God knows, if I had it to do over again, so many things I would do differently. Not just in my relationship, but in education, ministry opportunities, business ventures, and almost every facet of life. But as the old saying goes "hindsight is always 20/20."

I'm not saying don't self-reflect, but it's counterproductive to be more focused on your mistakes than the lessons they can teach. Learn from them and accept the way things are. Regardless of your dilemma, you will never be able to change the past. Why punish yourself for something you cannot change? When you forgive yourself, you're free to even apologize for any wrong you have done, because you have accepted that you are not perfect and you were bound to make mistakes.

When you understand how you cannot change your past, you should recognize that you are not responsible for the actions of other people.

While going through the difficult journey of divorce, the first lesson I had to learn is this, I was not responsible for my ex-wife's actions or decisions.

My Heartbreak, Pain, and Disappointment

I had known her since we were eight years old. We met in Mrs. Cook's second grade class. I remember those pigtails. She sat to my right. In third grade, our teacher was Mrs. Sparkman. That year, she had an ear infection. I was too young to actually know what that was but I wondered what was wrong with her ear. In fourth grade, it was Mrs. James and Mrs. Masters. Mrs. James was our main teacher but we also took an accelerated course a few days a week. We called it "gifted class." I'm not sure if that's the technical term. In fifth grade, our teacher was Mr. Gosa. We laughed for many years together about the time when he got so mad that he threw a chair at the wall! Sixth grade, Mrs. Ellis was our homeroom teacher. Seventh, it was Ms. Christian. Eighth grade was Mrs. Johnson. I vividly remember that year because this other boy had a crush on her. He was known for dancing and singing. On her birthday, he sang to her in from of the class. Everyone clapped and woo'd. I though he did ok!

Ninth grade was the first year since we had not shared the beginning of the school-day together since age eight. I noticed. She did too. We did, however share P.E. and Mr. Odom's math class. I would walk her to class after P.E. but never more than that. I wanted to make a move but she had a boyfriend at the time.

Tenth grade, I finally mustered the courage to let her know how I felt about her. I had left my math book in my locker and Mrs. Johnson instructed me to share with a neighbor. That neighbor just so happened to be the love of my fifteen year old life! Without hesitation, I pulled her desk next to mine. Her small physique made the action effortless but in that moment I seemed so strong. She blushed. I forgot my math book every day after for the remainder of that year.

We began courting, "liking" each other at age fifteen. As seniors in high school, we were an official couple. We were the "it couple."

My love for her was beyond explanation. I began preaching at age seventeen and she was the daughter of a preacher. She knew what to say to help me navigate through my unique experience as being a teenager, with all the lusts thereof, and being a man called of God to deliver His Word. She knew how to deal with a preacher outside of the pulpit because she grew up with one. The way she was there for me during my early stages in ministry made me love her even more.

After graduating high school, we both moved to Birmingham for college. She attended U.A.B. and I attended Birmingham-Southern. The ten minute distance between us only added to our inseparability. We spent time together every day. When I was nineteen, I popped the question on Valentine's Day. She satisfied me and I wanted to spend my life with her.

Looking back on the night I proposed, I can tell that we were not on the same page. Although she said "yes", there was a hesitation. How I missed that, I'll never know. But when you're in love, you miss all the warning signs. Red flags are only red flags if the relationship fails. Otherwise, we would have called them trials or mere bumps in the road.

We got married two years later (had to save up for the wedding she wanted). With approximately six hundred in attendance, we tied the knot. Our wedding had three photographers, and every picture brought joy to my heart. Nobody on earth could have predicted the shocking news in store five years down the line.

One day I left our home to go to a funeral at my church (I say "my" church as in stewardship and not ownership), I returned to an empty house. My wife and her family had moved all of her belongings out of the house. All of her clothes, furniture, decor, washer, dryer, light fixtures, rugs, tables, chairs, and even the dog. Now she had not come home the night before so I wasn't expecting her to be there. We had rough times and she wanted a break. But I didn't know that she wanted to leave me, let alone clean me out. I say all of her belongings, but all of *our* belongings would be more accurate. The only furniture left was the pieces that represented us: our bed and a loveseat. A bed but no marriage. A loveseat but no love.

To pour salt in this gaping wound, the church I pastored at the time was also having trouble, and this day it had reached a climactic peak. The deacons were upset with me and they wanted to meet with the church to vote me out as pastor. It was such a mess that I decided to go to my parents' house, an hour and a half away, and just lay on the couch. I did just that. I had to get away from it all. One of my trustees called me around seven that evening and said "Brother Pastor, they said you were voted out. But don't worry, we will fight because it wasn't done right. If we have to get a lawyer and go to court, we will fight it." I calmed him down and assured him that God makes no mistakes, people do. And many times we fight to keep what God is delivering us from.

What I didn't tell him was that my wife had just left me and I could give a *you know what* about being a pastor at that moment. Excuse my tone, but please understand that I would have given my left arm for that woman. I loved her that much. Losing her overshadowed any other loss, especially one where I had to fight to keep. The horrible news of losing the church was actually a great relief as it was less drama I had to directly diffuse. I loved those people. But I had grown weary of the constant arguing, bickering, and complaining. Have you ever heard the phrase "that's enough to make a preacher cuss"? Well that happened!

The quarrelsome church would have been easier to endure if I had a strong support system at home. Perhaps the marriage breakdown would have been less stressful if I had a loving and strengthening church experience on Sunday morning. But to leave a fight to fight again and return to fight some more left me without strength. I knew something had to give but it was impossible to choose. I didn't want to leave the church. I had done that before and vowed to never do it again. I refused to leave my wife. In spite of our personal problems, my love was unconditional. So I chased two rabbits and ended up with neither.

I continued to lay on my folks' couch, no one had made it home yet. I prayed for God's peace. After an hour, I got in my car to go back to my home in Birmingham and face the music. When I attempted to start the car, it stalled. There was no gas in the tank. I was so distraught that I forgot to stop by a gas station on my way to my parents' house. I didn't even recognize either of the two warnings my car gives when the fuel is low.

In one day, I had lost the woman I loved since my youth, I lost the church I labored to revive, I lost possessions I enjoyed, and my car had run out of gas!

How ironic an example of how life feels after you've been through something traumatic, like you've run out of gas.

To make matters worse, I didn't know why she left and I didn't understand why the church folks refused to give me a chance. Didn't she know that I needed her and she needed me? Can't they see the progress of the ministry? Can't they see that I need them and they need me?

Ok maybe, just maybe the church would see my personal life falling apart and show some affection and love. Or maybe my spouse would see my ministry blazing with strife and she would offer consolation until I got myself together. But that didn't happen. I don't even know if for better or worse crossed her mind. I learned why David prayed in Psalms 3 "Why are they increased that trouble me?"

My mentor said something that summed up this experience, "It's hard to be needed and not wanted." For this book, I want to alter that by saying it's *heartbreak* to be needed and not wanted.

You may wonder what exactly happened in the breakdown of our marriage. Truth is, I've chosen to not share those painful details and that's the way it will stay. But in summation, we had an empyreal love crippled by immaturity and lack of appreciation on both sides. Eventually, our sweet dream became a beautiful nightmare.

In the following weeks, I heard every rumor imaginable. I had beat my wife. She caught me with another woman. I had stolen money from the church. I had a criminal record I was hiding (that's why I use my first initial instead of my first name). The gossip mill was that I was a crook, an abusive husband, a failed leader.

The sad thing was that my wife and her family were the source of many of these untrue accusations. Talk about hurt. I mean if you want to leave me, just leave. That's painful enough. But why in the world would you lie on me? Why slander my name?

No, I wasn't the perfect pastor. Sure, mistakes were made. But God showed the ministry so much favor. Why embellish the truth? Why so much animosity?

I've discovered that people will ruin your reputation to save theirs.

No matter how disappointed you may be, don't dare retaliate. Revenge is reserved for the Lord. He said vengeance is mine. Don't hinder your blessings trying to do what God has promised to do for you. No matter how hurt you are, never get tired of being the bigger person. Don't allow that anger to corrupt your spirit.

I've experienced hurt and pain. I'm here to tell you that you can get through it.

Forgiveness is Hard, but Necessary

When you get a cut or a wound, an antiseptic is applied to clean out the wound and prevent bacteria from spreading. Often, the antiseptic will sting worse than the cut itself. But without it, the chances of the wound becoming infected are much greater.

That's what forgiveness does. It cleans out the wound so it can properly heal. It will hurt to forgive, but it prevents infections in your spirit and stops the injury from negatively spreading into other areas of your lives.

This is why I don't understand why people think that forgiveness is an attribute of the weak. It takes tremendous inner strength to forgive.

Revenge is the easy way out. It feels good for the moment but you don't get a consequence pass just because you were hurting when you did something. If that were the case, many people locked away in prison would be free today. There is no plea of not guilty due to temporary despondency. You can't lash out because you're infuriated by pain. Control your actions and forgive.

Forbes magazine has listed being a pastor as one of the most stressful jobs in America. Two of the most devastating challenges that a pastor can face is going through a divorce and being voted out of a church.

I was stressed and devastated times two. So no matter how heartbroken you are. No matter the disappointment. No matter the guilt or shame. I know how you feel.

But what we must learn to do is first is let the hurt and pain go. You have to forgive or it will weigh you down.

You can go higher when you get lighter. Let it go.

Closure For You

Closure is having a question answered. It's harder to forgive and let go when you still have questions. I understand. So let me answer a few questions for you in a way that helped me.

He will not apologize. She is not coming back. He will not send you that final text message to explain his feelings. She will not correct the rumors. He will not call you one night asking for forgiveness. She will not give you the truth you deserve. He will not remember the good times. She will not give it another try. He has moved on. She is happier without you. He has found someone else that he thinks is better than you were. She will continue to lie on you if she is pressed to tell the truth. He wanted you to suffer. She wanted to ruin you. He meant for it to hurt.

In Genesis 37, Joseph's brothers betrayed him and sold him into slavery. But he forgave them and let it go. They didn't know that by pushing him in a pit they were shoving him toward his destiny.

What the devil means for evil, God can make it good. Don't repay evil for evil. When life hands you a setback, focus on a comeback. Don't let the hurt break your spirit.

Chapter 2

You Are Not Alone

"...fear not: for they that be with us are more than they that be with them" 2 Kings 6:16

Have you ever noticed when you buy a new car, you start seeing other cars on the road that look like yours? When you spotted that car on the lot, you bought it in part because "not many people have one like this." As soon as you left the dealership, they seem to come from out of nowhere. Now unless you drive a Ford C-Max or something, you know what I'm talking about.

Well, that's how I felt when I got a divorce, minus the exciting feeling of car shopping of course. But the realization of just how prevalent it was. And just how typical my story happened to be. I read somewhere that between forty and fifty percent of marriages end in divorce. I also read that ninety percent of marriages are to a high-school sweethearts.

Although that last statistic hasn't been proven and many are skeptical due to current marriages happening at an older age median than in decades past, the theme is true that an overwhelming majority of married couples dated in high-school. But even those marriages divorce at the same rate as couples whose relationships originated otherwise.

I also found that divorces among pastors and ministers were at the same rate as divorces in general. The divorce rate in the church was the same as the divorce rate outside the church. Also, twenty-five percent of current pastors had been divorced.

Although these statistics are disturbing to say the least, I must admit that reading them and hearing about them gave me a sense of relief. It felt good to know that I was not the only one riding around in this car. There were so many others riding in that pain-mobile.

Let me pause and say this. If there is any chance, any hope, any ounce of possibility that you can save a marriage, a relationship, a partnership, a friendship, a kinship, etc., please put your pride aside and do whatever it takes to make it work.

Lord knows I did. I can honestly live with no regrets about my divorce because I tried everything humanly possible to work things out. She was not willing at all. I wouldn't wish that hurt and pain on anyone in the world. If you can save it, if you can make it work, God is truly a God of restoration. He can fix anything, but first there must be a willing mind.

But in the cases of total failure, irreparable breakdown, no hope or chance, please understand that you are not the only one who has endured that same trial. You're not the first and you won't be the last.

Don't allow the enemy to shame you into a hole, hiding from the rest of the world. You are not divine, you do not bathe in holy water, you do not use anointing oil as moisturizer, you do not travel to work by wings, just like everybody else, you are a human being. Which means you will make mistakes. No matter how good someone looks on the outside, they have made mistakes too. Although you may have some things to repent from, or to heal from, you do not have anything to be ashamed of.

The scriptures says that "There is now therefore no condemnation to them which are in Christ Jesus" (Romans 8:1). God separates us from our past faults and failures as far as the "east is from the west." One pastor illustrates so well that if our sins were as far as the north is from the south, then that would be counter-productive. If you travel north, you will cross the north-pole and if you keep going in the same direction, you will start going south. Keep going and you will pass the south-pole and begin to go north again. North runs into south.

But if you go east, and continue to go east, you will only go east. East never meets west. The only way east can run into west is if you turn around.

It's important that you are always moving forward from your pain, without regret, shame, or fear. God has fixed it so that your past will forever be separated from your future. You just can't turn around.

Closer Than You Think

I live in Birmingham, Alabama but I have a mentor who resides in Cincinnati, Ohio. He and his wife are like parents to me. They loved and encouraged both me and my ex-wife from the moment they met us. I felt like I could talk to him about anything but I was too ashamed to tell him over the phone. I wanted to tell him face to face.

One Wednesday, I got in my car to drive to his church service. I hadn't told anyone that my wife had left except my parents and one of my deacons whom I trusted and I knew he would lift me in prayer. As I was making the seven hour journey from Birmingham to Cincinnati, I received a call from a fellow preacher.

He and I had become close friends over that past year as we were serving at churches literally blocks from each other. When he called, he asked, "Man is everything ok with you and your wife?' (At this time, my ex-wife and I were having extreme marital problems about a month before she decided to move out and call it quits. This call was before she moved out, while things were still sort of private.)

I began to share with him what was happening and he told me that I would be just fine. I said "man how can you be so sure?" He replied "Baby boy, believe it or not, you are not alone. My ex-wife (he spoke of her by name) put me through the same thing when I was your age."

Now I had known this preacher and his wife for about six years. He has a beautiful family. A handsome well-mannered teenage son and a precious set of twins. He loves his wife dearly and you rarely see one of them without the other. They complement each other so well and almost twenty years of marriage later, you can tell that they are still very much in love.

But I never knew that he had been through a divorce.

He began to share his story. The heartbreak, pain, and depression he felt when it happened to him. Although it was twenty plus years ago, I could hear the hurt in his voice. First for the young lady. You don't expect certain things from the person you pledge your life to. Secondly, the grief of what could have been. Sometimes the possibility of what the future held is harder to let go of than the pain of the past.

But most of the hurt I heard in his voice was his sharing in my grief. I could tell that he hated that I was going through that storm more so than he did that he went through it himself. True friends can feel your pain.

It was amazing how similar our situations were. Seemingly the perfect young couple. In ministry. Serving as pastors of churches. Enduring the pain of separation, divorce, and public humiliation. Although decades apart, the devil is still playing the same cards as in the days of Adam: attack the man by attacking the marriage.

His testimony gave me so much hope. I admire this brother for the great work he and his wife are doing in ministry. I applaud the example they are to families and couples, young and old alike.

At that time, I held the belief that it was possible for my wife and I to reconcile. God is able to restore. But it was in that moment that I realized that even if my marriage didn't work out, I could still fall in love, have a beautiful family, lead a successful ministry, and find the strength to move on.

The point of this little story is to highlight the fact that I was driving seven plus hours to Cincinnati, Ohio just to find someone to talk to who would understand and not judge me or my wife for what we were going through. But turns out, help was right around the corner, literally a few blocks around the corner.

God will always place people in your life to help lift you when you've fallen. Don't forsake the people in your life. God has magnetized them to you.

Dust settles

Bad news spreads like wildfire. Some people thrive off rumors and lies. People tend to repeat what they hear without ever checking the validity of the source or subject. Tempers flare. People say and do things they didn't mean to say or do. Things get out of control.

But always remember that you don't have to respond to everybody who has something to say about you. You have to wait until the dust settles. It always does.

Remember when everybody was talking about Martha Stewart? Or Toyota Camry's? Or Magic Johnson? Last I checked, Martha was still baking and creating, Toyota Camrys are still ranked among the best-selling cars, and Magic is still Magic!

You have to let people talk. You are just the subject for the moment. The flavor of the week. You don't owe anyone an explanation for your life's decisions and choices. Focus on you.

Chasing down every rumor and lie only stirs up the dust. Let them talk. In the end, the chatter won't matter.

Come out of hiding

God created Adam and Eve in a pure and free state. Adam was commanded by God to not eat of the tree of the knowledge of good and evil. God also told him to instruct his mate, Eve, to not eat of the tree as well. Adam relayed the message, but Eve was led astray by a serpent and she ate from the tree. She then convinced her husband to do the same.

A beautiful young lady once told me that a guy messaged her on social media and asked "Can you be my Eve?" I told her to reply "I already have an Adam, so you must be a snake." Be careful who you entertain. I thought I would just throw that in for free.

Back to the story. When Adam ate from this tree, the scripture says they realized they were naked and covered themselves in fig leaves. Something interesting happened next. God began to look for Adam. "Adam, where are you?" God asked. But Adam was in the fig trees, hiding.

One pastor said that Adam had to be in fig trees because he covered himself with fig leaves. Fig leaves are larger than the fig fruit itself. The fruit is often even hidden behind the leaves. Adam and Eve had covered themselves with these large leaves in attempt to blend in with the fig trees for shame and fear of the wrong they had done. We do the same thing. We attempt to hide ourselves when we feel guilt or shame.

When I became single, at first, I tried to hide in a group of single guys, hoping that no one would notice my broken heart. If you're not guilty then I'm sure you've noticed how people often group themselves together because of their collective success of failure. But I submit to you that a lot of people are hiding because of fear.

There are future CEO's hiding on jobs where they are not happy because they want to blend in. There are ladies who will be role-models that are hiding in a promiscuous and provocative lifestyle trying to blend in. There are teenage geniuses and leaders who are constantly in trouble because they want to impress their peers, trying to blend in.

But Adam, God didn't call you to blend in with the fig trees, he commanded you to have dominion over them. Why are you trying to blend in when God called you to stand out?

Stop hanging around people who identify with your pain only. Find some people who identify with your passion and purpose.

And don't you dare shrink into a little bubble where you are alone and blocked off from the rest of the world. The enemy is strongest when you are isolated.

I'll admit, I was guilty of hiding, but only for one moment. I have a strong social media presence and when my ex left, I deactivated my accounts because I didn't want to be bothered. But that only lasted one day! I faced it head on. I realized that God was not pleased with me ducking and dodging because I was ashamed.

Truth is, you have nothing to be ashamed of. Whatever faults you have are between you and the Lord. If you don't remember anything else, please get this, you don't owe anyone any explanation for the decisions you make.

Third Wheel

Although I was separated, had filed for divorce, I didn't want to lose sight of my goal to one day fall in love again. It's easy to give up on something after a bad experience. As a remedy, I started to hang out with a group of married couples on Friday nights and holidays. All the times when they would meet and everyone was boo'd up, I came alone. It was extremely therapeutic in so many ways.

One, I got to see people who had been married, divorced, remarried, etc. still enjoy each other and live holistic lives. Second, I got to hear their' stories. I learned so much about relationships and marriage just by listening to them. Third, I was able to be corrected on some of my misconceptions. My marriage failed so obviously I wasn't perfect by any means.

Although often difficult to hear, I appreciate the sharpening and retraining of my relationship and marriage mindset. Forth, I learned what type of women to avoid by watching how these women were with their husbands. They also shared how they were when they first met. Fifth, I learned what it means to "be ready." Of course it means different things, but they all lead to the same, you're either ready or you're not. There are so many more lessons I've learned by being the third wheel.

One of the couples was my preacher friend and his wife whom I mentioned earlier. Because he could identify with what I was going through, he would call me often and say "Baby boy you need to get out of that house and come hang with us. You don't need a date, just come through and have a good time." He became my "wounded healer." I am forever grateful.

This is why I am writing this book. I want to help you heal. I want to let you know that it is possible to be greater than you ever were in your past. You can gain far more than you lost. Surround yourself with people who are proof of that and it will help you on your journey. With an example to follow, you will be reassured that pain is always temporary and trouble don't last always.

Whatever you went through, don't hide from it or hide because of it, embrace it. It's a part of your story but it is not the end of your story. God used somebody else's misery and turned it into a message so that I could be encouraged to keep going. I will do the same for you. You will have to do the same for someone else.

The scripture says "they overcame by the blood of the Lamb and the word of their testimony (Revelation 12:1).

Allow your devastation to be an inspiration. You are not the first to endure and you will not be the last. You are not alone.

Chapter 3

Half Full

"Now there were four men with leprosy at the entrance of the city gate. They said to each other, "Why stay here until we die? If we say, 'We'll go into the city'—the famine is there, and we will die. If we stay here, we will die. So let's go over to the camp of the Arameans and surrender. If they spare us, we live; if they kill us, then we die." 2 Kings 7:3-4

Perspective is everything. One of the first things I did after our relationship fell apart was create a new song playlist. I listened to a few songs over and over again, every morning when I got in my car. Some days, several times throughout the day. Kirk Franklin's entire "Nu Nation Project" album ministered to my soul. "There's a Blessing in the Storm", "He Loves Me", "Smile Again", "Love", "You Are", these songs gave me life.

One song in particular stood out and became my new theme song, "There Is a King In You" by Donald Lawrence. I played it to remind myself that in spite of my setbacks and challenges, God made me to be a King, a ruler, one with dominion.

The first verse goes:

> *"You come from royalty,*
> *An aristocratic dynasty.*
> *The goal of the enemy,*
> *Is that you don't know who you are.*
> *There's power when you speak.*
> *Be mindful of words you release.*
> *I know that life has challenged you,*
> *But the King in me speaks to the King in you.*
> *You were born to rule.*
> *There is a King in you."*

In all honesty, I was at the lowest moment of my life. I was so depressed I could feel it in my bones.

You know how you can feel love and joy? That warm fuzzy feeling. Happiness has a rather exciting feeling. Fear has an anxious or nervous feeling. Well depression has a feeling. Your body becomes numb, sometimes cold. Your legs feel like they are in an acupuncture session. Every morning I would feel it so strong. I didn't want to get out of bed.

I needed to change my perspective. I was in such despair that for the first time in life, I could smell the bones of dead dreams as I found myself at the crossroads of faith and mediocrity. For a split second, I contemplated being normal.

I often say that the thing I hate about being gifted or anointed is that anointed people make everything look easy. People don't realize the high price of great gain. Yes, I had seen God bless my life in major ways, but never without a cost. In that moment, I imagined living a regular life with a regular job and regular problems.

But I refused. My ministry couldn't die. My goals and dreams couldn't die. The vision for my life couldn't die. I have a mantle to carry. I'm the curse breaker for my family. There are generations counting on my innate resilience. Regardless of the challenges, there is something so great in me that God could trust me with this trouble. There is a King in me. By faith, this too shall pass. I will not be an average Joe. Before I die, even the devil will know that the Lord was on my side.

No Pain, No Gain

When you lift weights, your muscles are torn in the process. They become sore. That soreness is proof of gain. As the muscles repair themselves, they increase in size and strength.

As it is with the natural, so it is with the spiritual. When you are ripped and torn, you feel pain. But that pain is actually promoting strength and increase. You become more spiritually developed because of what you go through.

We often think that when we experience trials and tests that it is punishment. Although sometimes our troubles can be consequences of our own actions, the end result can still be positive and beneficial if we allow the blow to cause us to grow.

Adversity and Affliction

Isaiah 30:20 states that God will give you the "bread of adversity and the water of affliction." Water is essential to human existence. Our bodies are up to sixty percent water. Bread on the other hand will increase your weight. Eat a lot of bread, gain weight. Eat less bread, lose weight.

God uses adversity in our lives to increase our spiritual weight. We become heavier spiritually. Without life's adversities, so many things could easily knock us over. But because of the things we go through, we are not so easily moved.

People often say that tough times make you stronger. There is truth to that. But I believe that tough times also prove the strength you already have.

Maybe you were spiritually drained and emotionally scarred, but the good news is you were strong enough to survive.

In Acts 27, the Apostle Paul was on a ship that encountered a great storm. The vessel was ripped and the people on board had to make it to the shore by their own means. Those who could swim made it on their mastery. Those who could not swim made it by holding on to broken pieces and debris from the ship while they waded to the shore.

One pastor says that there are two types of people. First, those who can swim. Sure, problems come, but they are prepared to face them by their mastery and skill. But the second type is the survivors. They don't have a lot of training, but somehow they still make it, even if they make it on broken pieces.

After all I've been through in life, somehow, I always tend to land on my feet. I know that to be the grace of God. Through it all, I'm a survivor.

Without a doubt, God will allow us to go through certain things in life to strengthen us and to show us just how much inner strength we have.

Isaiah also states that God will give the "water of affliction." There are many uses and needs for water. But I believe that it is used here to illustrate cleansing, more specifically, spiritual cleansing.

When we experience some affliction in our lives, we clear out things that hinder our spiritual walk. We increase our spiritual and Christian activity.

We pray more. We go on a fast. We let go of some unhealthy relationships, habits, or communication. We go to church more. We spend more time in the Word. We focus on our spiritual walk with God in a more sincere way. Most importantly, we develop a greater sensitivity for the voice of God.

Most times when we fall into trouble or make a mistake, it's not because no one told us right from wrong, but we refused to heed sound wisdom. We thought our way was better than what we were being told.

My great grandmother passed a few years back. In preparation for the eulogy, I asked each of her children if there was one lesson that stood out the most from what Mama Lindy taught you, what would that be? One of my great uncles told the story of how he had to walk around a pond in order to make it home. One particular day, he didn't want to take the long way around the pond, instead, he wanted to cross the pond on a log.

He tried, even though everyone told him not to do it. Midway across, as predicted, he flipped over and fell into the water.

When he finally made it home, Mama Lindy had a great life lesson for him. She said "sometimes the longest way around is the shortest way home."

After that day, he became instantly wiser. That lesson stayed with him for many years and has saved him a lot of heartache and disappointment. It all happened because he fell.

What lessons have you learned from the stress you've endured? In life, we must learn to always look at the cup as half full. Even after a failure, tragedy, or setback, God is able to use that for the greater good. More importantly, God wants to make sure you don't make the same mistake again.

When someone gets a tattoo, the tattoo artist draws the pattern on the person first. Then he or she uses a needle to make the image permanently stick. The needle is painful, but it is necessary for the drawing to remain.

That's what affliction does. Although painful, it makes lessons stick. There are some mistakes that I will never repeat. Not because I didn't enjoy the activity, but I hated the lasting consequence far more than I enjoyed the temporary pleasure.

Sometimes, we have to be pressed. When there are wrinkles in your clothing, you press them. When wine is produced, grapes are pressed. God will not waste your pain. There is a lesson and a blessing in your pressing.

My Mother's Cup

My mother was raised by her maternal grandmother. She grew up in the south while my grandmother lived in Iowa. I don't know the full story of why my grandmother chose to allow my great-grandmother to raise her first-born daughter and I don't care to know. It was never a topic of family discussion.

As I got older, I could tell that it bothered my mother somewhat. She never verbalized it, but some things you can sense. My mother was her firstborn. My grandmother had two other children after her and she chose to keep them. Being the firstborn to my mother and father, I could not imagine the heartbreak and the confusion I would feel if that were my story.

When my mother was in her mid-forties, the family went to Iowa to funeralize one of my uncles. I was asked to perform the eulogy. After the service, we gathered at a relative's house. The older, more mature crowd huddled inside the home while the younger, more rowdy crowd corralled outside.

Like at most family functions, there are at least three different coolers. One with water and juice, one with sodas, and one with celebratory beverages!

The water cooler was near full, the soda cooler was half full, but the alcohol cooler was empty and being refilled! My family was drinking and having a good time.

After about an hour or so, there was loud commotion. It sounded like arguing and fighting. I figured another group of people had come to our family's residence to disturb our gathering. How disrespectful. Now I'm no fighter, but my uncle had just passed and if need be, I was going to tap into a Peter anointing! Blood is thicker than mud where I'm from.

But when I walked outside, to my surprise, there was no other group or family, but my family members were fighting against each other! The young men my age started taking their shirts off. I heard one of them yell "I'll mess somebody up. I just got out of the joint." I saw him run to his car. He shouted "F' it, I'm getting my gun."

His mother ran out from behind the house with her hands in the air screaming "Who the "h" is messing with my baby? You don't know me. I will send all you to the emergency room." She was around my mother's age.

I was shocked at the chaos I witnessed after a funeral. A funeral! Just hours earlier, these same people were leaning on each other in tears and grief. Now, they were acting like it was just another day in the hood.

I was standing there next to my mother and I noticed a calm look on her face. I don't know for sure but I felt she was thinking the same thing I was thinking.

All those years spent wondering why? All those years of disappointment and bitterness. All that hurt and pain. And this is what she missed! God knew exactly what he was doing. When I saw that foolishness, I thought "Those young brothers could've been me. That lady could've been my mother." But God saw fit to separate her from that.

God always knows best. He knows the end from the beginning (Isaiah 46:10).

This made it was easier to forgive my ex for the hurt and confusion she caused when she left. Maybe God was allowing me to experience this now to save me from something in the future. You never know what God is shielding you from. Ralph Waldo Emerson said "the years teach us much that the days never knew." We can see down the road, but God sees around the corner, and beyond.

My Father's Cup

When I was ten years old, I met my dad's father for the first time. He had been out of my father's life for many years. From what I know, he left for Chicago when my father was a boy and never came back. Again, not a frequent topic of family discussion.

That day, we rode to Chicago searching for him for what seemed like six hours. I remember my father asking people

"Do you know [him]?" calling his father by name. Several people seemed to know who he was but were unaware of his whereabouts.

Finally, someone settled the case and we waited by my grandfather's apartment for his return. Without an ill word or harsh tone, my father embraced the man who had walked out on him when he was a boy.

We've never spoken about it, but I am most proud of my father for the way he taught me supreme forgiveness. I can't imagine the pain he must have felt thinking that daddy was coming back home but he never returned.

I reflect on my father's number one attribute in my life, presence. Although my father was extremely young when I was born, he and my mother were both just eighteen, he has been there at every phase and facet of my life. I never had to wonder "where is daddy?" Birthdays, sports games, band, school meetings, home every night, recreational activities, vacations, rain, sleet, hail, or snow, my father was there. Even though I'm grown and gone, his support remains. Ministry, college, marriage, divorce, good days, bad days, whatever the case, I can count on him to be right by my side.

He didn't learn that trait by a great example from his father. I love my grandfather dearly, but he was not there. My father was and is in my life because he learned a lesson from the pain he endured. In the end, he's a better father, I believe, because he knows the harm it could cause when a father is not in a child's life.

My Cup

I began to serve as a church pastor at the age of eighteen. My pastor at the time had left the Baptist denomination to establish a non-denominational ministry. After I accepted the task to serve my first church, he told me in his living room that he would not be able to mentor me anymore. He couldn't be my pastor since he was moving away from the church where I served (which was my home church, the same church he resigned from) and cutting ties with the Baptist denomination. He instructed me to "find someone else."

At the time, I wasn't offended. I figured that it would be easy to find another pastor who would love to take a young pastor under their wing. To my surprise, this was more difficult than it seemed.

I contacted a few pastors that first year simply saying "I need a pastor. I need a mentor. Will you help me?" Their' responses were like they were reading from the same script. "Give me your number and I'll call you" and they never did. "We will do lunch someday. I would love to help." But the lunch nor help ever came.

After I poured out my heart to one of those pastors in a confidential meeting, he stood up in bible study the next night and made fun of one of the statements I made. Now he didn't call me by name, but there was no other young pastor who had a church in Sumter County who attended Birmingham-Southern. So I gather he was talking about me. That was a tough pill to swallow. I went to this man for help and this is what he chose to do. I wondered why no one wanted to help me. I was just a teenage boy preacher trying to do a grown man's job.

I began to hear rumors. Some preachers in the Birmingham area were discussing me. Wondering who I was. Where I had come from. If I really had a church or did I make that up. And most of all, what did I do to his pastor to make him disown him like that? They would talk down about me and criticize the things I did but never offered help or advice. I was never let into the inner circle gatherings. This was my bitter cup.

By this time, I was nineteen. I was essentially left alone to learn on the run. I had to teach myself how to baptize. I taught myself how to conduct communion. I taught myself how to prepare messages Sunday after Sunday. I taught myself how to administrate and how to conduct worship. And God blessed that church. I know it was Him because half the time, I had no idea what I was doing! But His strength was made perfect in my weakness.

For nearly five years, I served those people and many great things were accomplished. When I was twenty-three years old, I accepted the call to another church. It was an awesome opportunity. I went to preach there one time and they called me a couple weeks later telling me that the church wanted me to be the new pastor. I don't exaggerate or glorify numbers, but I say this for the sake of illustration.

This new church was double in everything. Double the property, double the membership, double the ministry, double the staff, double the facility, and double the pay, but of course, double the problems! That's another story for another day. I'm not saying that in a derogatory way toward that church. Some of my most precious memories are because of the kindness and generosity many of them expressed. But it is a truth, bigger ministries are sometimes bigger headaches. Be careful what you ask God for.

What amazed me was that when I got this "big" church, everybody started calling me "son." Son? Now I'm you're son? Where were you when I was crashing weddings trying to learn how to perform a proper ceremony? When I was collecting worship materials from other churches to study them to see how I needed to conduct a service? When I asked for help, I was talked about and even mocked. When I had a small rural church, you wouldn't even return my phone call. But now that my church is large, I'm your son.

Everybody wants to claim you when you make it, but never forget the people who stuck with you before your status changed.

It was a while before I found a mentor. Someone who would pour into my life and someone who I could be accountable to. But I am ever so grateful for the years in ministry where the counsel of the Lord made me strong. Where he granted me wisdom and favor in spite of my youth.

I have no malice against any preacher. But I will admit that it is hard to listen to guys now who shunned me then. I'm human.

I had to learn to see that experience as half full. I couldn't listen to the negative opinions of others. If that were the case, I would've quit the ministry a long time ago. But God wanted me to be different, so He comforted me in a way that no one else could. The exact reason hasn't been revealed to me yet. Maybe one day I'll mentor a great number of young preachers, because I know the pain of doing ministry without a mentor.

Maybe it was to strengthen my preaching. I started out preaching from explanation. As I matriculated through school, I learned how to look at the Bible in its original context and languages. I then began to preach from exposure and expertise. But after God allowed trying times to come, and I then learned to preach from experience. Experience is not only a good teacher, but a good preacher as well.

Whatever the reason, I trust that God knew and still knows exactly what He's doing in my life.

Christ's Cup

Before Jesus' crucifixion, He prayed earnestly to the Father. In anguish, sweat dropped like drops of blood from His brow. He cried "Father, if it be possible, let this bitter cup pass from me. Nevertheless, not my will. But thine will be done."

Jesus' cup was more empty and painful than any cup that either of us will ever have to endure. But He endured it. And maintained a proper perspective through that horrific ordeal, that this was the will of the Father. You must believe that same truth, that your bitter cup, whatever it may be, is all a part of God's plan.

Another favorite song of mine from the playlist I created was by Jessica Reedy. It's called "Better." The first verse goes:

"I used to be so broken, lost, empty.
A heart with no beat.
A singer with no song to sing.
So I know the feeling,
The silence is deafening.
But in your pain lies a blessing,
A sweeter song of victory.
So keep walking, walking, walking

Though it seems so far.
No it doesn't matter who you are.
See, there is one thing that I know.
Life it can leave,
You so bitter, bitter, bitter, bitter
But you must believe
That it gets better, better, better, better"

Don't lose faith or focus because of what you've endured. God will give you another opportunity, but you must have the right perspective.

Chapter 4

No More Slaves

"There is neither Jew nor Greek, there is neither bond nor free, there is neither male nor female: for ye are all one in Christ Jesus." Galatians 3:28

Let's play a little movie trivia. I wonder if you guess which movie this line is from:

"Imbrue. It means to taint, to stain. The cancer of racism imbrues our national character. It stains the spirit, taints the soul. It is a blot, a shameful greasy spot on the fabric of our national conscience."

This quote is taken from one of my favorite movies *Lean On Me* in which Morgan Freeman played the part of Principal Joe Clark.

Although slavery didn't begin in America, it certainly has had drastic effects on our history and even our present day.

Today, the idea that another person could "own" someone else and utilize them at their will seems ridiculous. It's hard to imagine how someone could be born and die without ever being free to make their own decisions about the basics of human life. The fact that society supported or allowed this to happen is even more perplexing. The idea of slavery seems to be far fetch, but is it really?

When my ex-wife decided to leave me, my first thought was simply "she can't." Without processing it, I thought that she, in a way, belonged to me and I to her. And that we could never leave each other because that's just what it was. I thought that we were eternally bound to one another by an unspoken rule of togetherness.

Boy was I wrong!

It hit me all of a sudden. I had developed a false sense of ownership. She was free to make any decision she wanted at any given time for any reason she liked. That was the reality that I ignored. We were husband and wife by relationship, but not ownership. Therefore, she was free to withdraw at any time.

The people in your life are loaned to you. Obviously, I wanted our marriage to last forever, but that didn't happen. I had to realize that any relationship is always a two or more person decision. You can't force anybody to do anything. There are no more slaves.

This portion of the book should teach you two things: one, if you have a relationship in which you feel that the other person "will never leave you", you may want to rethink that position. Always do everything in your power to make sure that they know that they are loved and appreciated. People need to be reminded that you want them in your life. Although that does not guarantee they will stay, but at least you'll have no regrets if they choose to leave.

Secondly, you should learn that you are not responsible for the decisions of other people. Never let anybody make you feel that something they decide to do is your fault. We are all responsible for our own actions, period.

When I was younger, I used to play the Madden NFL video game on Xbox. Up to four people could play at one time. There are eleven players on the field for each side, offense and defense. Someone is always the captain or leader for the team. But you as a gamer are only in control of one player at a time. On offense, it's the player with the ball. When the quarterback gets the ball, you're in control of him. Press one button and he passes to a receiver. Press another button and he gives the ball to the running back. Once the receiver or running back gets the ball, you are then in control of him and so on.

In life, you are only in control of one player, that's you. You can make demands, suggestions, give orders, make pleas, beg, shout, cry, or whatever you want, but ultimately you cannot control what another person decides to do.

Always appreciate the people around you. At any given moment, they could decide to discontinue the relationship. Never build an emotionally codependent life, ignoring the reality of human inconsistency. No matter the relationship, people are loaned to you. They are in your life for reasons and seasons.

Reasons...

You never know why God places people in your life. We can all share stories of how seemingly insignificant encounters led to a major breakthroughs in our lives.

When I was a junior in college, I was contacted by a recruiter at the Morehouse School of Religion. He wanted me to consider doing graduate studies there. I expressed to him that I wasn't interested at the time because I was serving at a church that was almost four hours away. I was also getting married that same year and my then fiancé was not a fan of relocating to that great a distance.

But the recruiter was rather persistent. He recommended that I visit Atlanta for a tour of the campus. I agreed to do so. During spring break, I was given a three day tour of the school. While at lunch, other prospective students and fellow seminarians were introducing themselves, stating their' names and credentials. The eight or so gentleman at the table were shocked to know that I was already pastor of a church and had been so for almost three years (I was twenty-one at the time). I remember them saying "I've never met a pastor so young."

This one preacher from North Carolina interrupted and said "I have. I know this preacher back home who is twenty-two." I had to find out who this preacher was.

My attention shifted. As I raised my brow, I asked "Who is he? Do you have his number?"

I shared earlier the difficulty of navigating through ministry without a senior pastor. That was coupled with the fact that I had no peers who were in my same shoes. When I started pastoring, the counterparts closest to me in age were in their mid to late thirties. Of course, in this line of calling, you're still a "young pastor" over into your fifties.

To hear that there was another pastor who my age was music to my ears. The gentleman gave me his number and I called him that day. After our first conversation, we hit it off.

We began to share war stories about pastoring at such a young age. We were quickly open and honest about our youthful mistakes and immature ambitions. We laughed together, at ourselves, and admitted rather quickly that neither of us knew what we had signed up for!

I was about to get married and he had just gotten married. Our spouses were equally happy that we found each other because it took a little pressure off them both. Now we had someone else we could lean on.

Six years later, we are the best of friends. We see each other in person maybe three times a year, but we talk almost every day, several times a day.

Although I never went to Morehouse, that experience led to me having a genuine friend.

During our friendship, he and I have both experienced divorce. He and I have both had financial difficulties. He and I have both been mistreated and falsely accused. He and I have both faced difficult ministry moments. Only God knows the things we've said to one another.

God placed us in each other's lives for a reason.

Seasons...

Our problem is not so much with the *why* someone is there, but *how long* they are. You never know the span of time people are assigned to share your life's journey.

When I was in high school. Like most people, I had a best friend. We both played on the junior varsity basketball team. Although I was tall, athletic, and I could dunk, I didn't get much playing time during games, neither did my friend. As a matter of fact, out of the ten players on the team, the coach really only played seven. This didn't bother my friend and I as much as it did the last guy on the bench.

During that basketball season, I learned something valuable. Sometimes, it's not your time to play in the game, but rather to support those who are on the court. I'll one day write a book entitled "A Season on the Bench: Waiting Until Your Time."

But my friend and I enjoyed that season. We made the best out of being benchwarmers. Of course we wanted to play, and we enjoyed when we had the opportunity to play, but ultimately it was up to the coach, and we were ok with that.

That experience brought us together. We talked on the phone every day it seemed, picked up girls together, went on double dates, hung out over each other's house, etc. We were the best of friends for a couple years.

When I started preaching, we drifted apart. We didn't fall out with one another. Never had an argument or ill word spoken. The relationship just wasn't the same. I don't think we drifted apart because I started preaching but rather because our season had ended.

We see each other from time to time. Every now and then, a Facebook message or comment. But I don't even have his number saved in my phone. Sometimes, that's the way life is.

People are in your life for reasons and seasons and we must learn to appreciate the times we share with those who are in our lives. Never feel that someone will be there forever. This point alone makes the experience easier. Whether it's divorce, death, drifting, disagreement, distance, or differing directions, most people are in our lives temporarily.

People Change

Why would you say "I do" to vows and act as if those vows never existed? How could you agree to the contract terms (for better or for worse, in sickness or in health, 'til death do us part) and not honor them?

I was so confused when she wanted to leave. We had both made terrible mistakes in or marriage, but I was so ready to spend the rest of my life with the woman I loved in a Godly and mature way. I had gotten to the place where I was ready to lead our marriage to the next level.

I had accepted responsibility for all I had done in the past and the way I made her feel. I even told her that I forgave her for anything she may have done. I promised to never hold anything over her head and cover and protect her if anyone else tried.

But she didn't want it that way. She wanted out. Initially, she would not apologize for any wrong. She began to spread vicious rumors and lies which left me even more confused.

Can I be honest? I really didn't understand the lies because the truth about our situation would have been degrading enough.

Not only was I confused, but I was utterly shocked.

I thought I knew this girl. I mean I've known her since we were eight years old! I had spent countless hours with her family. Every other weekend, for the first two years of our marriage, we would spend the night at her parents' home because of the distance to the church I pastored. We had been married for five years and were together five years before that. I thought I knew this girl.

Life has a way of teaching you that you never really know what someone will do. It's not easy to grasp, but sometimes people change.

Free Yourself

When a person detaches from you, you have to rid yourself of your attachment to them. The best way to do this is to focus on you.

Don't allow what they didn't see in you cause you to doubt yourself. I couldn't name a Taylor Swift or Blake Shelton song if you paid me. But I guarantee they don't care! My ignorance does not affect their' relevance. Your value is not determined by the people who don't recognize it, but by the ones that do. That has to begin with you. That's why it's called "self-worth" and "self-esteem." It's about how you view and value self.

I wrote earlier how I felt my pastor had abandoned me. There were moments in ministry when I didn't have a senior pastor to pat me on the back and tell me how good of a job I did. My spouse would tell me "good job." My parents would say "so proud of you." My peers would say "keep up the good work bro." But I've often wished that one day he would pick up the phone and call and say "You have made me proud." That never happened and I've found strength to not let that bother me.

Please don't think that I'm speaking negatively of him. I believe with all my heart that he is proud of me and prays for me. The purpose of this whole chapter is to get you to realize that you and I cannot judge other people for the decisions they make. Whoever doesn't call or text, you have to learn to be ok with that, just as I learned to.

I've heard it said time and time again that "rejection is redirection." But I've realized that rejection can also be protection. Don't get upset when people change their minds and want to do something different than you would desire. It just may be God preparing you for something greater or protecting you from something worse, and quite possibly both.

When you learn to prioritize your relationship with God, it all makes sense. Why grieve the people who leave when you can embrace the God who stayed? He promised to never leave you or forsake you. If someone volunteers to leave your life, let them go.

Chapter 5

Gratitude

"In everything give thanks: for this is the will of God concerning you." 1 Thessalonians 5:18

The great tragedy of today's society is a sense of entitlement. Too often people are unappreciative because they feel like someone owes them something. That is not the case. This is why 1 Thessalonians 5:18 is one of my favorite verses of scripture, "In everything give thanks: for this is the will of God concerning you." I'm reminded that everything in my life is gratitude worthy. Even the undesirable or hurtful are subject to the will of God.

I want you to look at your situation from a different angle. Not only forgive whomever harmed you, but to also thank them and thank God for them.

Although my marriage ended, I had to thank my ex for all the good that she had done. I thanked her for all the lessons she taught me. I thanked her for all the sacrifices she made. I could not allow the last season of our relationship to cast a dark cloud over the truth, I appreciated what she meant to my life and ministry.

Have you expressed gratitude for what you lost? Have you thanked that person for sharing a part of life with you? Or do you feel like you did them a favor?

There comes a time when you have to mature beyond the blame game and embrace the facts. They had to do something good because you were with them. Some positive quality or trait drew you in and kept you there. Even though it didn't turn out like you wanted, you must admit that something good did come out of the relationship. For that, be grateful.

I wrote briefly about my last church and how things didn't work out. But when I look back at the situation, I can't help but be grateful for the experience. There were so many laughs and great times. I witnessed the Lord move and work in a way that I hadn't before. I learned so much about myself as a leader and administrator. Most importantly, I learned so much about people and the pastor/pew relationship. I can't say that I have gotten it all right, but I do appreciate the experience.

I've also mentioned the challenges I've faced without my pastor guiding me. Although it's easy to be bitter, I can't overlook the eighteen years prior to that time when he nurtured and covered me spiritually. Even though he didn't have a direct influence in my public ministry, it was because of him that I was strong enough to handle the task.

He made sure that I could recite passages of scripture by heart from age nine. And not just the twenty third Psalm and the Lord's Prayer. He made sure that I learned the books of the Bible and could recite them forward and backward. He made it possible for me to gain exposure at a very young age. He had a heart for youth and he and his wife worked tirelessly to make sure that we had a strong foundation. That foundation is what I stand to preach from. For what he instilled in me, I am forever grateful.

It's so easy to focus on the pain that we forget the good.

Even though my ex walked away and didn't want to come back. I'm grateful for her. Even though my last church gave me a pink slip. I am still grateful for them. Even though my relationship with my pastor ended. I am still grateful for him.

Times Like These

Separation and divorce brought on a great deal of challenges for me. I struggled financially. My reputation had taken a hit and my character was in question. Depression had invaded my life. Fear and anxiety attacked my mind.

I was lied on, ridiculed, falsely accused, falsely arrested, restrained from my home, judged, and counted for dead.

My friend from North Carolina immediately wired me some money. I never asked or made it seem like it was needed. The preacher I mentioned earlier who had suffered a divorce in his early ministry offered me a room in his home, gave me the codes to the alarm, and keys to come and go as I pleased. He allowed me to use his garage for storage until I sorted things out with the judge (which I did two weeks later).

After I left the last church, I was led to start a new ministry called the Galilee Missionary Baptist Church. Most of the members of Galilee were also a part of the last congregation. When I left, they left. They knew what I was dealing with personally and they decided to stick with me.

I am most proud that during my times of struggle, they showed me so much love. As a matter of fact, they had a special day for me and called it "Love Day!"

These people made sure that they prayed for me and kept me encouraged. They showed so much grace during this time. There were times when I couldn't even finish a message, but they responded as if it was the best sermon they had heard. I could write an entire book about the greatness of these people alone.

What I'm stressing is that you really don't find out who loves and cares for you until life gets hard. Anybody can love you when money is flowing and people are calling your name, but who's there when all of that is gone? It is a true saying that "tough times reveal true friends." When you recognize who they are, always find a way to let them know that you appreciate them.

Patti Labelle faced media scrutiny for showing a lack of appreciation. A viral video turned her little known sweet potato pies into an overnight success. When asked about her pies selling out of stores in one weekend, Patti responded "My pies were selling out before the young man did that video." She went on to say "I did all the work." That was not the case. Before that video, the pie was virtually unheard of. After four million views, over a million pies were sold in one weekend. The number would have been much higher but they were sold out everywhere. Patti was right. She did do all the work Therefore she deserved the credit. But the video did help her pie sales, therefore, she should have shown the gentleman some appreciation. Not long after her media faux pas, she invited the gentleman into her home and began to publicly thank him for his contribution in her pie selling success.

God alone is worthy of the glory. You can get the credit. But there are people in your life whom you should show appreciation.

I am grateful for the tough times. They revealed real friends, but more importantly, they revealed the real me. While I was undergoing tremendous stress and trials, I became proud of the person of faith that I had become. Yes, I became proud of me.

Notice I didn't say I had "pride in me," but I was indeed proud of myself for the way I reacted. I never knew I had that much strength. I was previously unaware of the amount of integrity and character that I had developed.

If you would be honest, you really surprise yourself when you think about how you responded to all that you endured. Sure, mistakes were made, we're only human, but considering the circumstances, things could have been far worse.

The Apostle Paul writes in Philippians 4:8 *"Finally, brethren, whatsoever things are true, whatsoever things are honest, whatsoever things are just, whatsoever things are pure, whatsoever things are lovely, whatsoever things are of good report; if there be any virtue, and if there be any praise, think on these things."*

Regardless of your set of circumstances, think on the good. I've discovered that the more you think, the more you thank. Be grateful.

Chapter 6

Proceed With Caution

"Look carefully then how you walk, not as unwise but as wise, making the best use of the time, because the days are evil. Therefore do not be foolish, but understand what the will of the Lord is." Ephesians 5:15-17

NBA great Kobe Bryant's stellar career has been plagued with injuries. Several surgeries have caused him to sit out a considerable amount time. But with a naturally competitive spirit, he was always anxious to get back on the court sooner than recommended. I'm sure if he could have, he would've suited up and played even while hurting.

However, his medical professionals knew that although he felt good and that he could very well play a good game, if the injury was not completely healed, the chances of further damage are greater. Even at ninety percent recovered, you're still injured.

This is a lesson I learned the hard way. After our separation, my heart was ruptured. I felt every emotion possible. I prayed earnestly for God to heal my broken heart and He did.

As my heart began to heal, as I approached ninety percent recovery, I thought I was ready to date someone new. Maybe even fall in love again. Or at least have a good time with someone I admired. But contrary to the advice of my mother, I tried. I realized quickly that I simply wasn't ready. Mama was right, I was moving too fast.

It's not that I was hurt by anyone else, but that the heartbreak was not out of my system. One day as I was cleaning the house, I decided to listen to some R&B. I turned my Pandora to the Babyface station and why did I do that!

I might as well asked for all the R&B songs ever made about a man missing a woman. He was singing "Do I ever cross your mind... anytime? Do you ever wake up reaching out for me?" I muscled through that song like a champ thinking it would get better, but Pandora is messy!

The next song went "When can I see you again? When can my heart beat again?" I rushed to change the station! I just wanted some good smooth R&B. I quickly pressed next and a commercial came on so I went in another room to finish what I was doing.

While my mind had gotten away from the radio, a Boyz to Men song came on, "Although we've gone to the end of the road, still I can't let go. It's unnatural. You belong to me, I belong to youuuuuu....." and that's where I lost it!

I ran to the bed we once shared and began to cry "I want my baby!" I am not ashamed to admit! I sung that whole song to her even though no one was home but me. Boyz to Men is a quartet group with four part harmony and I sung every part! I was Shawn, Wanya, Nathan, and Michael all at the same time!

It had been about four months since we'd been apart. One of my friends had moved on so quickly after his divorce that he remarried before the ink was dry. He is now happily married for almost twenty years. I thought that I could do the same. But even after four months, it was like she had just left that morning.

Although I thought I was ready to move on and it had been a while since I had an emotional fit, all it took was a little 90's R&B to show me that I was still wounded.

Trust me, those feelings do go away. That pain does subside. That wound does heal, but it takes time.

Now I can listen that same "break-up music" and smile. I can relate to the lyrics and enjoy the artists' expression while reminiscing on the good times. I noticed that while riding home from church and Jaheim's song "Back in My Arms" began to play. The chorus ends with "you're still my lady if only in my heart."

His words were so true to my experience. That's me who still has that photo in my wallet. And wondering why we ever fell apart. But listening to that type of music this time around was a different experience. I was getting better. No tears formed.

I know it feels like the pain will never stop. But indeed it will. Keep pursing purpose and believe that every day will get better.

Healing Takes Time

When I was a boy, I hurt my knee while playing outside. The pain was excruciating. The worst I had ever felt. I was taken to the doctor for x-rays and they showed no major damage. I was told that my knee would heal in no time. I was given a pair of crutches and a knee brace. My instructions were to stay off my knee so that it could repair quickly and properly.

I enjoyed that. I could sit around the house with my leg propped while everyone catered to me. "Pass me the remote. Bring me a sandwich. I'm under doctor's orders to rest and not put any weight on my knee."

This is why the people in my life were telling me to not move too fast. When it comes to injuries of the heart, it's important to "stay off" that damaged place until you recover. Getting back in the game too quickly can set you back beyond your original injury.

You can't operate at the same capacity when you're hurt as you could when you are whole.

Regardless of social or peer pressure, admitting that you may not be ready is not a sign of weakness, but of maturity and humility.

Denial is the first stage of grief. To think that you are ready to do something only to realize that you're not proves that you are in a season of grief and that you need time to heal. Trying to be macho-man or superwoman will only fool you, everyone else knows that you're hurt. Let your loved ones cater to you while you heal.

Guarding Your Heart

Proverbs 4:23 says *"Above all else, guard your heart, for everything you do flows from it"* (NIV). Your heart is the muscle of your human spirit. When your heart is healthy and whole, so will your life be. When your heart is broken and tender, it will affect everything around you.

When you realize that your heart is not fully healed, separate yourself from harmful atmospheres and negativity. It can cause more damage than the original wound.

Chapter 7

Do Something Deeper

"Behold, I will do a new thing; now it shall spring forth" Isaiah 43:19

Luke chapter five tells the story of the calling of the Apostle Peter (then Simon) into the discipleship ministry of Jesus Christ. Jesus had just finished teaching and Peter was heading back home after an arduous night of fishing where he caught nothing. Jesus says to Peter "Launch out into the deep and let down your nets for a draught." Peter responds "Master, we've toiled all night and caught nothing, nevertheless, at your word I will let down the net."

I'm grateful that Jesus stayed on that boat with Peter even though he had failed at what he was doing. He had caught nothing. But Jesus never looks at us for what we are, He sees what we can be. Although Peter had failed, he wasn't a failure.

Failure is always an event, never a person. Therefore, Jesus stayed with Him and pushed him to succeed. You should never dwell on people who leave you because there are no "fish in the boat." Real love will appreciate the effort even when the results are not what was desired. Real love will try again.

Jesus told Peter to launch out into the deep. Seems to me that Peter was fishing in shallow waters when Jesus wanted him to go deeper.

Many times in life, we gave up when things didn't work out the way we planned. But we ignore the bases that we left uncovered. We don't self-reflect on our own inadequacies and shortcomings in a way that reveals what could be if we tried the same thing again in a deeper way. Jesus wanted Peter to fish again, but not in shallow water. Go deeper.

I've often heard people say that they have given up on love because of what has happened to them. For me, this is not the case. Maybe I was fishing in shallow waters. Maybe I didn't go deep enough. Maybe there is another level that I had not attained.

My ex and I started dating at seventeen and were married at twenty-one. Quite naturally, we made youthful mistakes. Due to our age and immaturity, although our love was real, in retrospect, it was shallow. That's not a detriment to either of us, it's a truth about where we were in our stages of development.

There are some things that I did with her that my next wife will never have to worry about. I'm sure we have all said it "If only I knew then what I know now." That's a good place to be. Learning and growing from what you've been through so that the same mistakes won't be repeated.

I heard a story about this young preacher who was intent on impressing the crowd. He walked with his chest out as he strutted to the pulpit. His every motion was to call attention to his expensive jewelry and exotic shoes. When it was his moment to preach, his braggadocios tone was obvious. He demanded that the people clap, stand, and cheer. He was filled with pride for his ability to spark a crowd.

Halfway through his message, the people were tired of looking at him. In spite of all his flash, his message was bland and confusing. It was clear that they were eager for him to sit down. He soon ended the message with great humility and reverence for the task that he miserably failed at. Afterward, he said to one of the older ministers "I had them up shouting and clapping from the moment I stood up. How did I lose the crowd like I did?" The old preacher responded "If you would have started like you finished, then you would have finished like you started. Next time you get the opportunity, preach the same sermon but start from the last page and go backwards."

In a classroom, the teacher teaches the lesson and then administers the test. In life, it's just the opposite. You're tested and then taught. But, you will always be tested again. No one expects you to pass a test that you've never studied for, but after the last failure, you should have learned some lessons that would prevent you from repeating the same.

I can't turn back the hands of time, neither can you. But you can begin today living life on a deeper level.

Invest in You

The best time to invest in oil is when stock prices are low. I've learned that the price of a certain product is not always a representation of that product, but usually an indication of the market's response. The law of supply and demand states if there is a low supply and a high demand, the price will be higher. In contrast, the greater the supply and the lower the demand, the price will be lower. Essentially, the price does not affirm or downgrade the value of the product, it simply adjusts to the market.

The same is true with you and I. After a bad break-up, we feel like our *stock* is low. We feel like damaged goods. And in many cases, we are damaged. That season can be the best opportunity to spend time working on you. One writer's advice to all single people is simple yet profound; 'build your body, your brain, and your brand."

Body, Brain, Brand

Our physical health is always important to maintain, especially during times of great stress and hardship. Stress can have negative, even fatal effects if not properly managed and treated. I made my local gym like a third home (second to my church). I don't consider myself to be a professional body builder, but I realize the importance of staying in shape and how doing so positively affects my emotional well-being. When we work out, we look better. When we look better, we feel better. And the energy is continuously transferred.

Conversely, allowing that stress to fester can have consequences on your appearance and health. You want people to say "You don't look like what you've been through" and not "You look like you've been going through!"

Building your brain is simple, you have to read. You have to expose your mind to other ways of perceiving and dealing with your issue. It's an awful statement to say "the way to hide something from us is to put it in a book."

Reading improves your memory, increases your knowledge, refines your focus, reduces stress, and provides limitless entertainment. And it doesn't matter what you read. It's like bench-pressing two-hundred pounds with a standard weight set or bench-pressing a two-hundred pound steel beam, it's the same workout. Two hundred pounds is two hundred pounds.

As it relates to mental stimulation, reading two pages of the sports section is just as effective as reading two pages of the business section. With all the material available at the touch of your finger, there is no excuse for us not to read every day.

Building your brand has a certain corporate overtone. Some may think this doesn't apply to you. But truthfully, we are all the *CEO's* or our own lives and destinies. No matter who you are, you have a brand to uphold. Everything you do represents the *brand of you.*

While going through a rough time, watch what you express and expose on social media. Once it's posted, you can't pull it back. Even when you delete it, it's still out there somewhere. Always project love, forgiveness, peacefulness, joy, and strength.

Also building your brand can be literal in the sense of business. There are plans and inventions that God has placed in you that the world is waiting to see. Your time alone can be well spent building your business and shaping your professional brand. It took the awful experience of divorce to pull the author out of me. As a matter of fact, I've scheduled more preaching and speaking engagements in the six months following my filing for divorce that I had done in the previous three years!

I'll be honest. When my ex left me, I wanted to crawl in a ball and hibernate. For a brief moment, I deleted my Facebook page and Twitter account. I turned off my phone and stayed locked in the house. But I had real friends who would not let that be. I came out of that hole and focused on rebranding.

I did a photoshoot with a smiling face and no wedding ring. I was depressed, saddened, broke and broken, but you couldn't tell! I began to post messages about forgiveness and love. Promoting joy in the midst of my pain. I knew that one day the market would change.

You Have to Overcome

In some cultures, when a child does something that would cast a negative light on the reputation of their family (like get pregnant out of wedlock or commit some horrible crime), the child is shipped off to an undisclosed location. Sometimes to live with other relatives or to a boarding school. The geographical distance provides a way of escape and an opportunity to work out problems without scrutiny or criticism. But most of us are not so fortunate. We can't pack up everything and just move, we have to overcome.

Your stock may go down, but it doesn't have to stay that way. Allow that rough patch to help you develop your body, your brain and your brand. The energy you waste trying to resurrect a dead situation could be better used investing in yourself. You can overcome.

The Civil Rights Movement of America is a perfect example. African-Americans couldn't pack up and move to Africa or someplace else, the only option was to overcome. They put the vision to music and the theme song of the movement became *"We shall overcome. We shall overcome. We shall overcome some day. Deep in my heart, I do believe, we shall overcome some day."*

Deeper in God's Word

I'd like to add to building your brain, body, and brand: get in your Bible! *"For man shall not live by bread alone, but by every word that proceeds from the mouth of God"* (Matthew 4:4). The greatest investment you will ever make is to deposit into your spirit. When you are fed a healthy diet of the Word, you become stronger and more mature.

Whatever you feed will grow over time. In today's tech savvy world, there are countless ways to be exposed to scripture daily. You can receive a morning Bible verse via text or Google a daily Bible reading. It's like taking a spiritual vitamin or doing a spiritual workout. The truths of God's Word will guide and guard you throughout the trials and opportunities of each day.

Deeper Relationships

In order to go deeper, you may have to evaluate the people around you. Sometimes in order to change seasons, you have to change circles. Everyone that starts out with you is not meant to stay.

When God told Abram (better known as Abraham) to leave his family in Genesis chapter twelve, Abram disobeyed and brought his uncle Lot along for the trip. Lot ended up costing Abram a lot! Abram learned a valuable lesson, you can't elevate higher than the people you surround yourself with. Sometimes, you have to separate to elevate. Bad company corrupts good morals (1 Corinthians 15:33).

Chapter 8

Las Vegas

"There is nothing better for a man, than that he should eat and drink, and that he should make his soul enjoy good in his labor. This also I saw, that it was from the hand of God." Ecclesiastes 2:24

I've always known my father to be a hard worker. He is the man who never takes a day off. He works as a mechanic at a local university where he and a crew maintain the college's vehicle fleet. He gets time off most days the college is closed (i.e. holidays, spring break, etc.). But even on those days, he finds a way to put on his work clothes and find somebody's car to fix. I've never known him to take a week and just relax.

I was one of those children who said "I will never be like my daddy and work all the time." But after ten years of ministry, it occurred that I was the spitting image of my father's occupational tendencies. I had never taken a vacation. I mean a real vacation.

Now I had traveled across the country several times, but mostly due to ministry assignments, church conferences, or the occasional funeral. But I had never taken the time to ride off to a distant destination, leave my suit and tie in the closet, and solely have a good time. I had to make this vacation count. So I boarded a plane and headed for Las Vegas, Nevada.

Ok, I did accept an opportunity to preach, but that was not the original plan. I even preached in jeans when I normally wear a suit. Let's be clear, no matter where I decided to vacation, I would still attend worship at a local church. I had also made up my mind that if I was invited to preach, I would accept the opportunity. One of my church members sent me a text and said I was breaking my rule of relaxing by doing any kind of work, but for me, preaching is always satisfying. The people of Second Baptist Church made me feel right at home. Dr. Chaney and Pastor Joe treated me like family and the experience will forever be a pleasant memory.

But I was determined to have as much fun as I could while I was there. I was a single man in Las Vegas! I won't detail all of my adventure because as you know "what happens in Vegas stays in Vegas!" (This is the part where I wish LOL was acceptable in book writing) It was a phenomenal trip. But I did have to change the nickname while I was there from Sin-City to Fun-City. It's important to note that it is possible to have fun and not sin.

I knew that there would be some people who would want to judge or comment on whether or not a pastor should be in Las Vegas, but that didn't matter to me. One great thing that this process has taught me is to never base your decisions on other people's opinions. Someone will always have something to say. I say all the time that if you put a thermostat on seventy degrees, someone will say it's too hot. If you turn it to sixty-nine degrees, someone will say it's too cold. You may as well set it to where you are comfortable because people will complain either way. In order to really enjoy life, you have to be delivered from the opinions of other people.

I have a relative who underwent a weight loss surgery. Several months after the surgery, although she had lost a considerable amount of weight, she still had a few extra pounds, if you know what I mean. If you saw her today, you may say that she is overweight and needed to get in shape, but she is convinced that she is one of the finest women that God has ever created. She dresses like she has the figure of a magazine cover model. Never afraid to show off her body as it has transformed after her weight loss success. I love that about her. Even though she is not where she may ideally want to be, she celebrates the fact that she is far better than she was. She is not moved by the opinions of others because they are ignoring the progress she has already made. People will judge your *after* when they don't know your *before*. If someone is critical about your presence, they are usually ignorant of your past.

That's why you have to live your life free of what others may say or think.

With Jesus Alone

On my trip to Vegas, I traveled solo. By this time, I had gotten used to sleeping alone, eating alone, encouraging myself, and enjoying my time with me. It's important that you learn how to enjoy yourself. If you're not happy when you are with you, how can someone else enjoy your company?

I read a scripture during my devotional reading one morning that changed my life. Exodus 36:13 "And he made fifty clasps of gold and coupled the curtains one to another with the clasps. So the tabernacle was a single whole." (ESV). The tabernacle was a portable tent used to house the very presence of God. In the designing of the structure, God's desire was that it would be a "single whole." Though many parts, they made one complete tabernacle. As it relates to the New Testament believer, our bodies are God's tabernacle and God has the same desire for us, that we be single, but whole.

When a man and a woman join together as husband and wife, it's not half a man joining with half a woman, but two whole persons joining together and allowing God to perform divine arithmetic, the two becoming one flesh.

I realized that if I was to be successful at being single, then I had to be just that, successfully single. This meant that I had to be happy with Jesus alone.

Who said that you just had to have somebody anyway? I mentioned earlier in the book about my group of married friends. Every Friday, we have date night. That's right. I go to date night every Friday with a group of married people and I'm the only single person there. I never feel awkward, out of place, or have any less fun because I enjoy being with me. Yes I bring a date from time to time, but it's optional and not a necessity. I've learned to embrace the fact that in this season of my life, God wanted me to be alone.

Alone vs. Lonely

Being alone is a state of being. Being lonely is a state of mind. God said that it was not good for Adam to be alone, so He created Eve. But Adam never complained about being lonely. Eve's companionship was God's choice at God's time. Adam was content with the way God made him and the work he was assigned to do. Daily Adam communed with God and he was satisfied. We have to learn to be alone and not choose to be lonely.

Erasing the feeling of loneliness is a process. It won't go away just because you want it to. I won't pretend as if I didn't experience that feeling. After the first days and nights alone, believe you me I felt lonely. I had to undergo companionship detox. I was with her for so long that when she was gone, my ears missed her voice, my hands missed her touch, my nose missed her smell, and my house missed her presence. No matter how many times I washed and mopped, Fabreeze and Gain could not compare to the scent of a rib.

My church family even missed her presence and her sweet spirit. Many of the members of my current church were members of the church that I previously pastored. They had grown to love her and they never got the chance to say goodbye. She changed her number so none of them were able to contact her to see if she was ok. We all grieved her absence and I felt lonely many days. Nothing was the same as it was before.

But I refused to let the lonely feeling get the best of me. It was quite natural for me to grieve the death of our marriage when you consider the depth of my love. The Bible says that "To everything there is a season and a time" (Ecclesiastes 3:1). But you can't hold your head down too long.

It was said that because a giraffe's head is relatively small as it relates to the size of it's heart it cannot hold it's head down for extended periods of time. The blood flow could cause the giraffe to collapse if it doesn't quickly lift its head up. The same is true for you and I. If we hold our heads down too long, it can cause a collapse in our spirit or depression and anxiety in our minds. Just life the giraffe, even though at times our heads are down, we must find a proper balance to keep us properly flowing.

Even if you feel as if no one else loves you, lift your head and love yourself. Loving yourself means than sometimes you will have to laugh alone, eat dinner alone, watch a movie alone, take a trip alone, enjoy your life alone, all while daily fellowshipping with God, just as Adam did.

When we look in Genesis 2, we also see that Eve spent time alone with God. When God formed Eve, He caused a deep sleep to come upon Adam. When God was ready for the two to unite, He brought Eve to Adam. If God brought her to Adam, she must have been alone with God while Adam was still asleep.

Building a personal relationship with God is not gender specific. Male or female, you are designed to know and love God first. Then you will always be satisfied with God's presence even if others become absent.

Fun Guilt

For me, having fun after heartbreak was somewhat of an awkward feeling. Almost like I was doing something wrong, no matter how harmless the activity.

Once I got past the general sense of loneliness came this new feeling. I call it *fun guilt*. As I began to go out and enjoy new experiences, I had fun, but deep down I wished I was sharing those experiences with the woman I pledged my life to. I was introduced to this new restaurant with some of the best Cajun food you can find and a live band every Friday night. I had a blast every time I went. I knew that she would absolutely love a place like that. My church members gave me a special day to show their appreciation and admiration. I was all smiles. But I was constantly thinking how much she would enjoy that moment. I went all the way to Las Vegas. Something that was totally out of character for me. I had so much fun while I was there, I knew that trip would have been a highlight of her life as it was for mine.

Honestly, that last night in Vegas, I couldn't sleep. Around three o'clock in the morning, I began to cry. Not tears of sadness, but tears of regret. I thought "Why did I never take her to Vegas? Maybe that one gestor would have made all the difference." Fun guilt is real, at least it was real for me.

God had to reveal to me that it was perfectly OK for me to enjoy life without her. I prayed that she was enjoying her life as well. When she left me, she decided to have a good life alone and I had to accept that and do the same.

You must expect enjoyment. Had I not gone through so much pain, I wouldn't appreciate the pleasures. Joy is the harvest of tears. Weeping endures for the night, but joy comes in the morning. Don't waste your morning by mourning. Jesus said that He came "that you may have life and have it more abundantly" (John 10:10).

Laughter is Medicine

Some traumatic experiences require professional counseling. Some may be helped by medication, either temporary or long-term. I am an advocate of those who seek licensed and certified help for healing. I believe that whether you are healed instantly, over time, with or without medicinal or professional help, your healing is a miracle nonetheless. If you need professional help, seek it and prayerfully follow the physician's treatment.

However Proverbs 17:22 states that "A merry heart does good like medicine." King Solomon in all his splendid wisdom made it clear, laughter is good for your health.

Studies show that laughter lowers stress, boosts your immune system, relieves muscle tension, and even increases blood flow to promote a healthier heart.

Aside from the physical benefits of laughter, there are psychological benefits as well. It can decrease stress, give you a better mood, lower your anxiety, and ease fears.

During my healing process, one of my favorite comedians was coming to town. Mr. Katt Williams himself. I'd never seen him perform live so I bought a front row seat. The show was hilarious and immensely therapeutic. I wasn't concerned about who saw me there or what they would think. I needed to laugh. I needed to heal. If you know Katt Williams, then you know that I cannot repeat any of his jokes in this book!

Most mornings, I go to breakfast with a group of older preachers, average age in the group is around sixty-five, including me! I glean a great deal of wisdom and knowledge from these seasoned veterans, but I must admit that I don't go for that. I go for the laughs! Our table is the highlight of the restaurant every morning. You ever go somewhere and there's this loud group at a table in the back? That would be us! Enjoying food, fellowship, and laughter. I wanted so badly to share a joke from the group, but I don't think old preacher jokes are appropriate for my target audience!

I will however share a couple from the comedian of our family. Remember I wrote earlier about the relative who had a weight-loss surgery? Well she's a vintage family entertainer.

Once she was asked, "Why did you feel you needed to have surgery to lose weight? What exactly made you do it?" She responded, "Well, all my life I've had a little extra meat on my bones. I've always been able to take good care of myself. But as I began to, you know, spread, I needed help doing everything. I had to get my children to help me put my shoes and socks on, help me take my shoes and socks off. My little boy was three years old and he already knew how to unhook a bra because I couldn't do it myself! But that didn't do it. What made me decide to have the surgery was one day I didn't have my children to help me put lotion on my legs. So I looked for the spray lotion but I ran out. I looked for some hair spray because my legs was so ashy and dry. But I didn't have that either. All I had was some Pam butter cooking spray and I figured it would work just fine. So I got my legs all nice and shiny and went on about my day. All of a sudden, I felt something crawling on my legs. Before I knew it, ants were all over my legs biting the heck out of me! After I got through spraying my legs down with the garden hose, I knew something had to change!"

Ok. If that didn't get you, I have one more and I'm done.

This same cousin had a best friend who also a little more to love. They were riding buddies and they are both queens of comedy. One day they were speeding down a highway and they were pulled over by the police. They looked at each other and one of them said "If we was little petite women, we could smile and he wouldn't even give us a ticket." Cousin said to her friend "Girl, we need to think of something quick, I don't need another ticket on my driving record. Start screaming now." The friend replied "Huh?" The officer was quickly approaching the car and cousin told her again "Start screaming." With the officer almost at the window, the friend began to scream as instructed. Cousin whispered "Put your hands on your stomach." As she grabbed her stomach, cousin rolled down the window and said frantically, "Mr. Officer, Mr. Officer. I am so sorry for speeding but my friend is nine months pregnant and she just went into the labor! Could you please escort us to the hospital in Meridian?" These gals got a police to escort them to a hospital outside of his jurisdiction just to get out of a speeding ticket! Tell me that's not funny!

Bottom line, have as much fun as you can. Enjoy yourself, enjoy your family, enjoy your church, enjoy your hard-earned money, enjoy your time on earth, and most importantly, enjoy Jesus.

Chapter 9

Relax, Reset, Recover

"And David was greatly distressed; for the people spake of stoning him, because the soul of all the people was grieved, every man for his sons and for his daughters: but David encouraged himself in the Lord his God. And David said to Abiathar the priest, Ahimelech's son, I pray thee, bring me hither the ephod. And Abiathar brought thither the ephod to David. And David enquired at the Lord, saying, Shall I pursue after this troop? shall I overtake them? And he answered him, Pursue: for thou shalt surely overtake them, and without fail recover all." 1 Samuel 30:6-8

In football, there's this play called a timing pattern. It's a passing play. The quarterback receives the snap and drops back about five yards to throw. Meanwhile, the wide receivers are running their designated routes preparing to catch a pass. The quarterback is not looing for a particular player, but he will throw to a specific spot on the field. The wide receiver's job is to make it to that spot. The best way to defend against the timing pattern is for the corner to hit the wide receiver at the line of scrimmage. This could possibly throw the wide receiver off his route or cause him to arrive at the designated spot too late. The defense knows they can't touch the wide receiver once the ball is in the air, which would cause a penalty for pass interference. Therefore, that initial blow at the line of scrimmage is of utmost importance to the stopping of the play's success.

In the same way, the enemy knows that God has a certain spot for you. God has released choice blessings into the atmosphere and He has assigned you to a certain route that will lead you to your place of great favor. The enemy knows that he is limited in his power, therefore he will deliver a hard blow to distract you from running the route that God has assigned.

Whenever you suffer a hard blow, you should rejoice because that's proof that God has sent your blessing priority mail. If I were you, I wouldn't let the devil stop me from running my route, from getting to my spot, from chasing after my dream, from believing God, from praying, from going to church, from lifting my hands in worship, because God has a reward for my labor, a blessing for my pressing, rest for my test, my weeping has endured for a night, but joy is coming in the morning.

Don't just take my word for it, let me show you how God proves this in His word. In 1 Samuel 30, we find the Psalmist David in a moment of mental anguish and psychological distress. As David and his men returned to their homes, they realized that the entire town of Ziklag had been raided and burned. Their' possessions stolen, their' properties flattened. To add to the terror of the moment, their' wives and children were kidnapped. Everything they worked to gain was gone. Everything they worked to keep was taken away. The men were so distressed that they wept until "they had no more power to weep."

Have you ever cried out? Have you ever cried yourself to sleep? Have you ever cried until you had no more power to cry?

How weak does one have to be to not be strong enough to pass tears? I know I'm not talking to everyone, but somebody knows exactly what I mean. Somebody can say "Pastor, I've been there." You tripping because I showed up late when I'm lucky I showed up at all. You talking about "those shoes don't match that belt" when after what I went through I barely noticed my right foot from my left. That's why you have to be careful when you put your mouth on people. You never know what the enemy has stolen from me. You never know how my life was just ransacked. If you knew what I had to face when I got home, you would lift your hands for me because you know just how down I am.

Depression is real. Separation anxiety is real. Grief is real. Loneliness is real. Low self-esteem is real. Unemployment is real. Divorce is real. Heartbreak is real. Bad reports are real. Disconnection notices are real. Is there anybody here dealing with something real? Some real pain. Some real stress. Some real deadlines. Some real decisions. This is not an excuse. This is not a pity party. Today, it just got real.

For David, things got as real as it could get in 1 Samuel 30. Don't give up on David just yet.

See, David was anointed to be the next King of Israel. But although he was hand-picked, he still had to wait to be promoted. King Saul still held the position even though God had rejected him. Some people have positions but no power. But that would soon come to an end because in 1 Samuel 31, the very next chapter, Saul commits suicide by falling on his own sword. In first Samuel 30, David is in trauma. But in 1 Samuel 31, David is in charge!

David, maybe the enemy is attacking you so hard in 1 Samuel 30 because in the next chapter, you're about to be elevated!

David, I know you were hit at the line of scrimmage in chapter 30, but keep running that route because you will complete the play in the next chapter.

I wish you would hear me child of God. This is not the last chapter of the story of your destiny. Keep running your route. Eyes have not seen, ear has not heard, neither has it entered into the heart of man the things that God has in store for them that love Him. Many are the afflictions of the righteous, but the Lord delivers them out of them all. And we know that all things work together for the good of them that love God and are called according to His purpose. Quit quitting, stop stopping, give up on giving up, for the race is not given to the swift, neither the battle to the strong, but to the one that endures until the end. Don't stop, get it get it!

David teaches us what to do when we suffer a major blow in life.

First, You Need to Relax

When their anger reached maximum capacity, the men needed to blame someone for the tragedy. Since David was the leader, the blame fell on him. The men were so that they "spake of stoning him."

The first reason you need to relax is because no matter the threat on your life, it's still just a threat.

Usually, words would carry more weight, but if the Lord wanted David dead, he would've died in the fire. But since you're still here, that must mean that God has a plan for your life that's inclusive of the enemy's plot. Let people talk about what they are "gonna do" and what they "wanna do". Let them chatter. When God gets ready to move, the chatter won't matter.

The next reason you need to relax is because the men wanted to "stone" David. This is not the first time we see David in a passage with stones. In 1 Samuel 17, David becomes a military hero by slaying the giant Goliath with a rag a rock. He packed five smooth stones for the battle, but due to the favor of God, he only needed one to bring down Goliath. Certainly, David's might and strength alone could not accomplish this feat, this had to be the power of God working through David and his stone.

My point is that God showed us with David and Goliath that even the stones are controlled by the hand of God!

There was no need to worry about the mean who wanted to stone David. God has power over stones. As a matter of fact, even if they upgraded to their spears, or swords, or javelins, or arrows, David would still be protected because my Bible says that "no weapon formed against you shall prosper and every tongue that rises up shall be condemned."

I don't know what they said to make you panic, but relax. I don't know what they did to make you afraid, but relax. God has power over words and weapons.

Second, You Need to Recharge

David began to encourage himself. The phrase "encouraged himself" in the original language means to strengthen oneself or to recharge.

When my phone needs recharging, I plug it into a power source. I wondered how David could recharge without having someone else to plug in to. Then I noticed that he encouraged himself "in the Lord." David had a wireless charger! When he was weak, the Lord made him strong.

I don't understand people who miss church because they are going through a tough time. That's the time you need to show up early. How can you expect to be refilled if you don't come to the filling station? In tough times, you don't run from God, you draw closer to Him.

I hear you. "David encouraged himself so I can too. I don't need to go to church." Keep reading. David also called for the priest Abiathar and asked to use his holy vest. David was obviously close to the priest. There are people that God has assigned to your life to lift you in times of crisis. Go to church, go to a conference, go on a retreat, and recharge. David encouraged himself in the Lord, but the connection came through the priest.

Third, You Need to Reset

David prayed "Lord shall I pursue?" God will never create a life for you that makes prayer unnecessary. When you realize that your plans, your goals, and aspirations have been interrupted, you must pray.

Prayer is like your reset button.

When I was a boy, my friends and I would play Streetfighter on Sega Genesis. I was pretty good and often won. Every now and then, the game would freeze. There was only one option at that point, to reset the game system and start over. If you were winning, you hated it because all your hard work was for nothing. But if you were losing, you were excited when the game froze and you were grateful for the option to reset.

I know you didn't like what happened to you, but be grateful that God can reset your life. David, I know you lost all of your resources, but you still have access to the source. When you reset in prayer, you realize that the same God who did it before is well able do it again.

Lastly, You Need to Recover

David was blessed to be reunited with the ones he loved. He got his family back. He got his stuff back. In the end, he was elevated to become King.

I can't tell you that you'll get your woman back. I can't say that you'll get your man back. I can't even say that you will get those possessions back. But I will say that you can get your swag back. You can get your joy back. You can get your peace back. You can get your wealth back. You can get your strength back. You can get your hope back. You can get your purpose back. You can get YOU back! You will recover all.

CONTACT THE AUTHOR AT

www.dfoyhutchins.com

Copyright © 2015 D. Foy Hutchins
All rights reserved. No part of this book may be reproduced, scanned,
or distributed in any printed or electronic form without permission.
First Edition: December 2015
Printed in the United States of America

Printed in Great Britain
by Amazon